This book is dedicated to
all the little people for inspiring me,
and all the BIG people for believing in me.

Copyright © 2020 Tiny Tinkles Publishing Company

All Rights Reserved.

No parts of this publication or the characters in it, may be reproduced or distributed in any form or by any means without written permission from the publisher.

To request permission, or for school visits and book readings, please visit www.tinytinkles.com

ISBN (Paperback Perfect Bound): 978-0-9808888-4-3

ISBN (Paperback Saddle Stitch): 978-0-9808888-0-5

ISBN (Ebook): 978-0-9808888-1-2

First Edition 2020

HOW TO READ THIS BOOK

Read the story. Have fun! Use silly voices and make animal sounds.

Talk about what you see. Music notes and symbols are scattered throughout the story. Point them out or ask your child find them for more learning opportunities.

Tiny Tinkles Little Musician books are designed to grow with your child. Pages and concepts in this book can be used independently or read from cover to cover in one sitting. Introduce learning and concepts as your child is ready.

TOOLS TO HELP YOU TEACH

Music Road – When you see the dotted line of Music Road, follow it with your finger or have your child follow it with their finger. Make your voice higher or lower as the line moves up and down.

Animal Friends – All the animal friends correspond to music notes and each has a special song. Point to the animal friends, repeat their note, or sing their song to reinforce music concepts and note memory.

Sing Alongs – When you see this star with the name of a song inside, you can sing along with a recording of the song. Go to tinytinkles.com to access the recordings.

For videos, worksheets, and other resources, please visit
www.tinytinkles.com

In a land far away,
there is a very musical place called
Tiny Tinkles Town.

Let's follow Music Road.
We will sing high and low,
and meet all of our new friends!

Music is all around.
Sometimes the notes are **short**,
and sometimes they are **long**.

tweet

kah

1

1 - 2

Everyone who lives in **Tiny Tinkles Town** sings their own special **song**.

mmm

hoooot

1 - 2 - 3

1 - 2 - 3 - 4

Chloe Cat sings along to Tina's lovely melody.

meow

 Find the letter C and the 𝄞 Treble Clef sign for high.

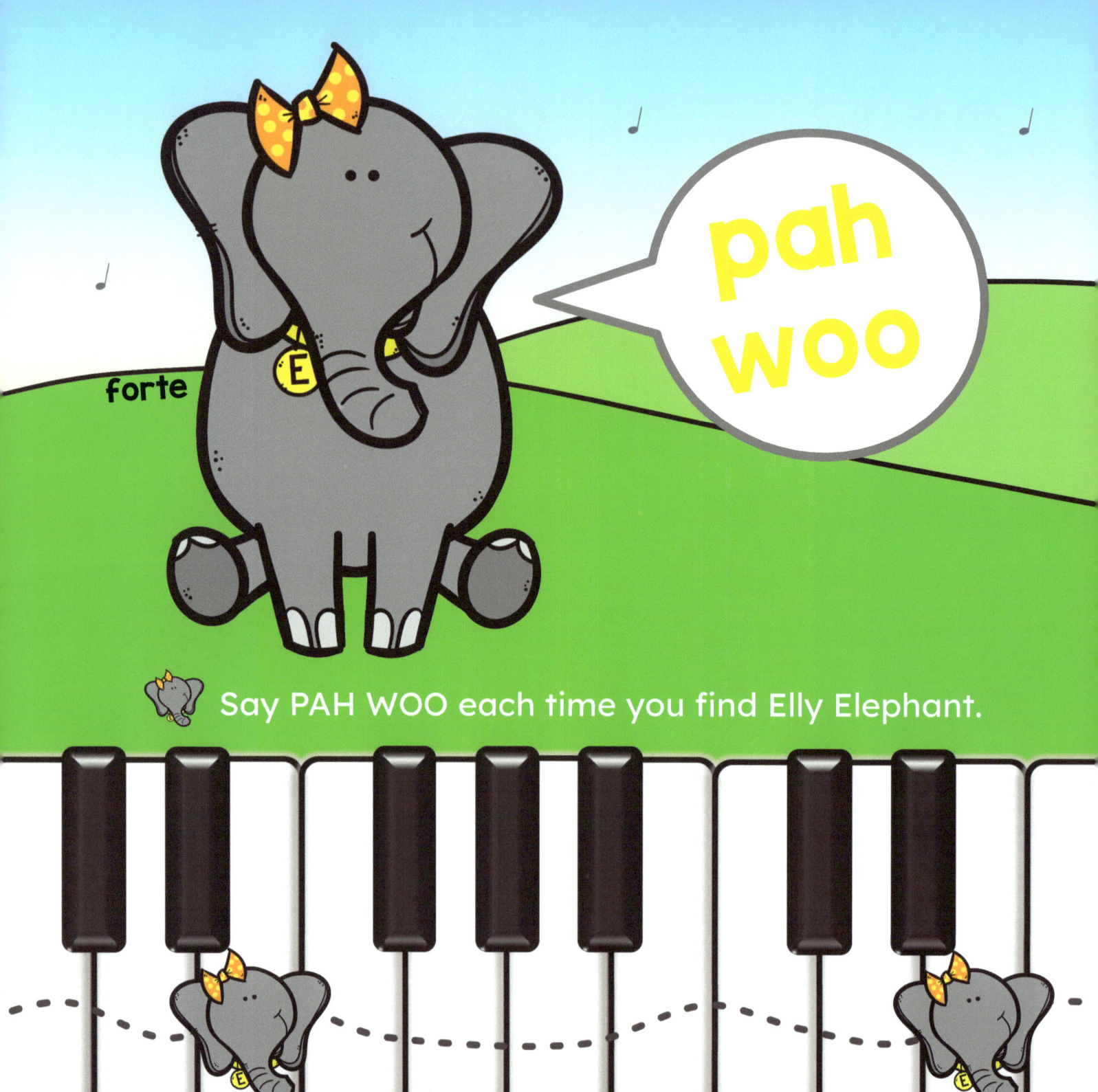

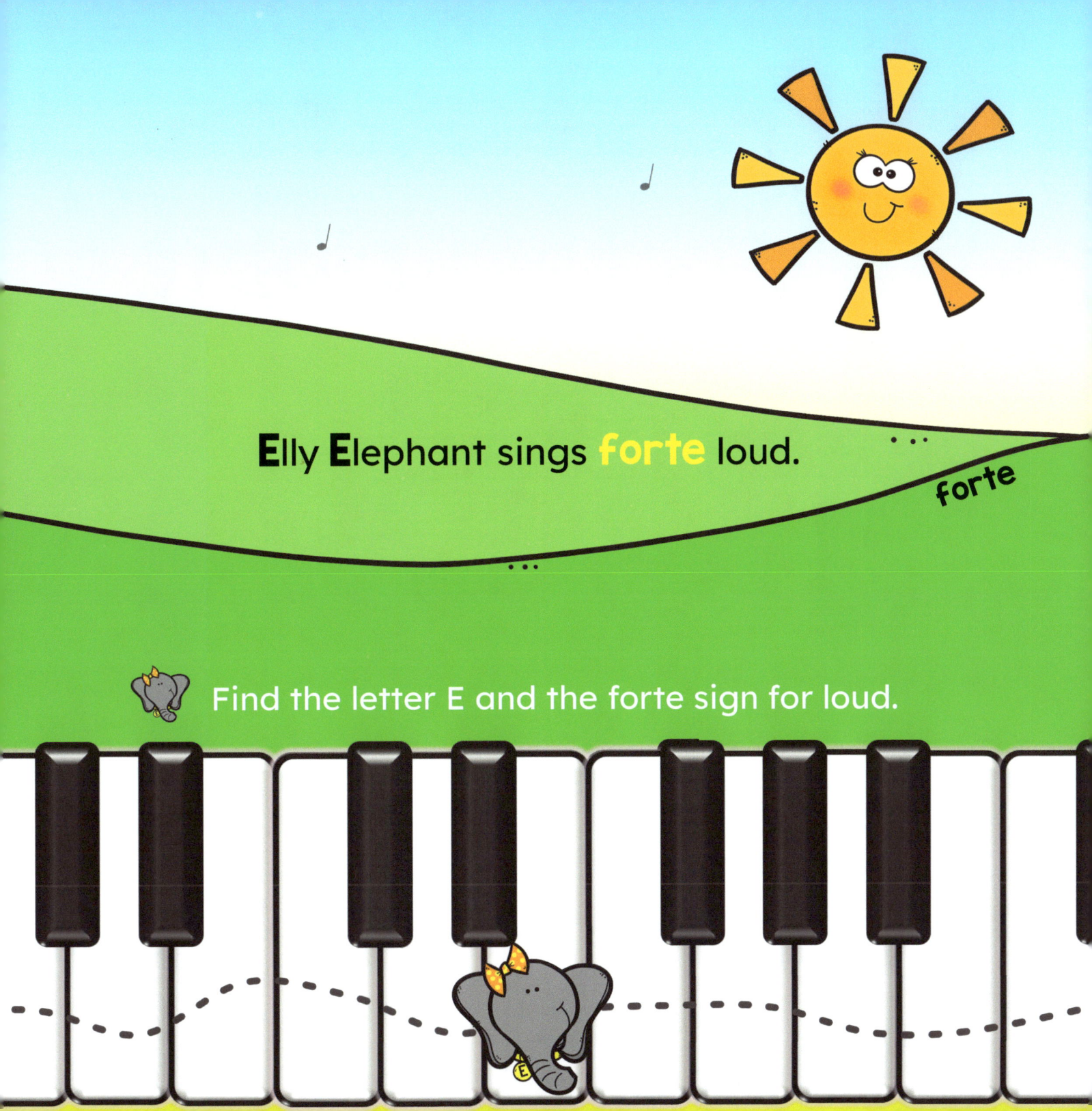

Franky **F**rog sings piano soft.

 Find the letter F and the piano sign for soft.

Gordie Goat sings **adagio** slow.

Find the letter G, and the slow whole notes.

Ally **A**lligator sings **staccato** short.

Find the letter A, and the short staccato notes.

Brownie **B**ear sings with the cutest little accent.

Find the letter B, and the notes with accents.

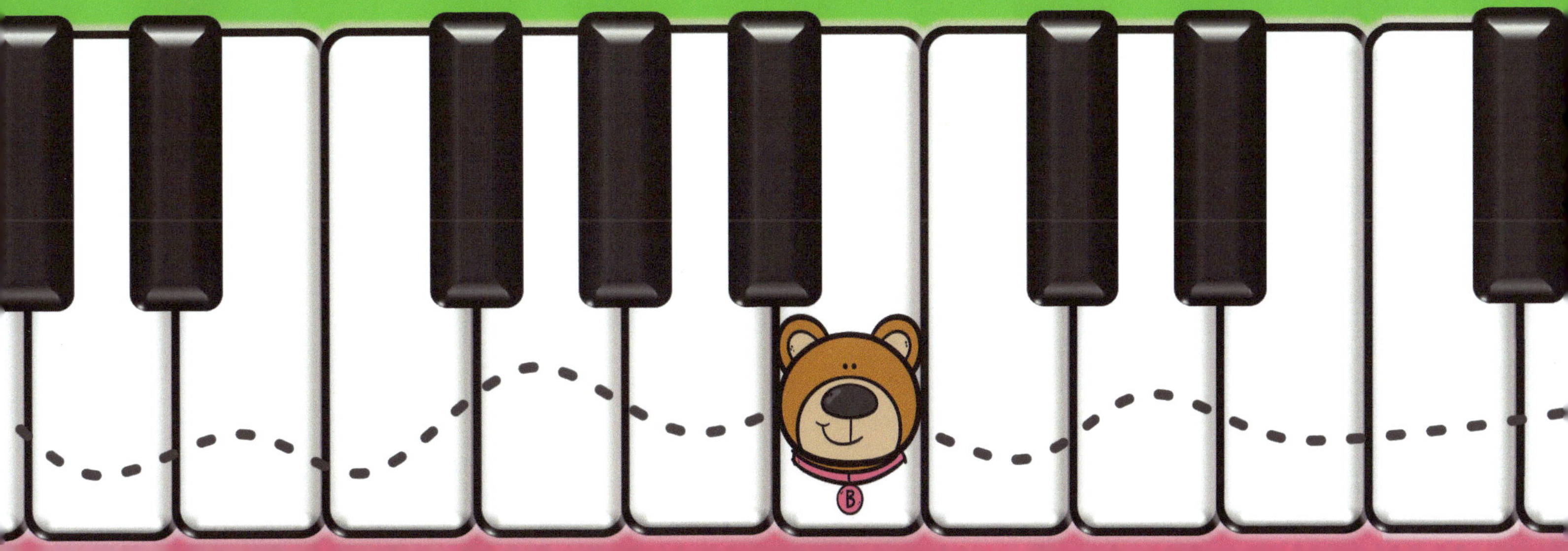

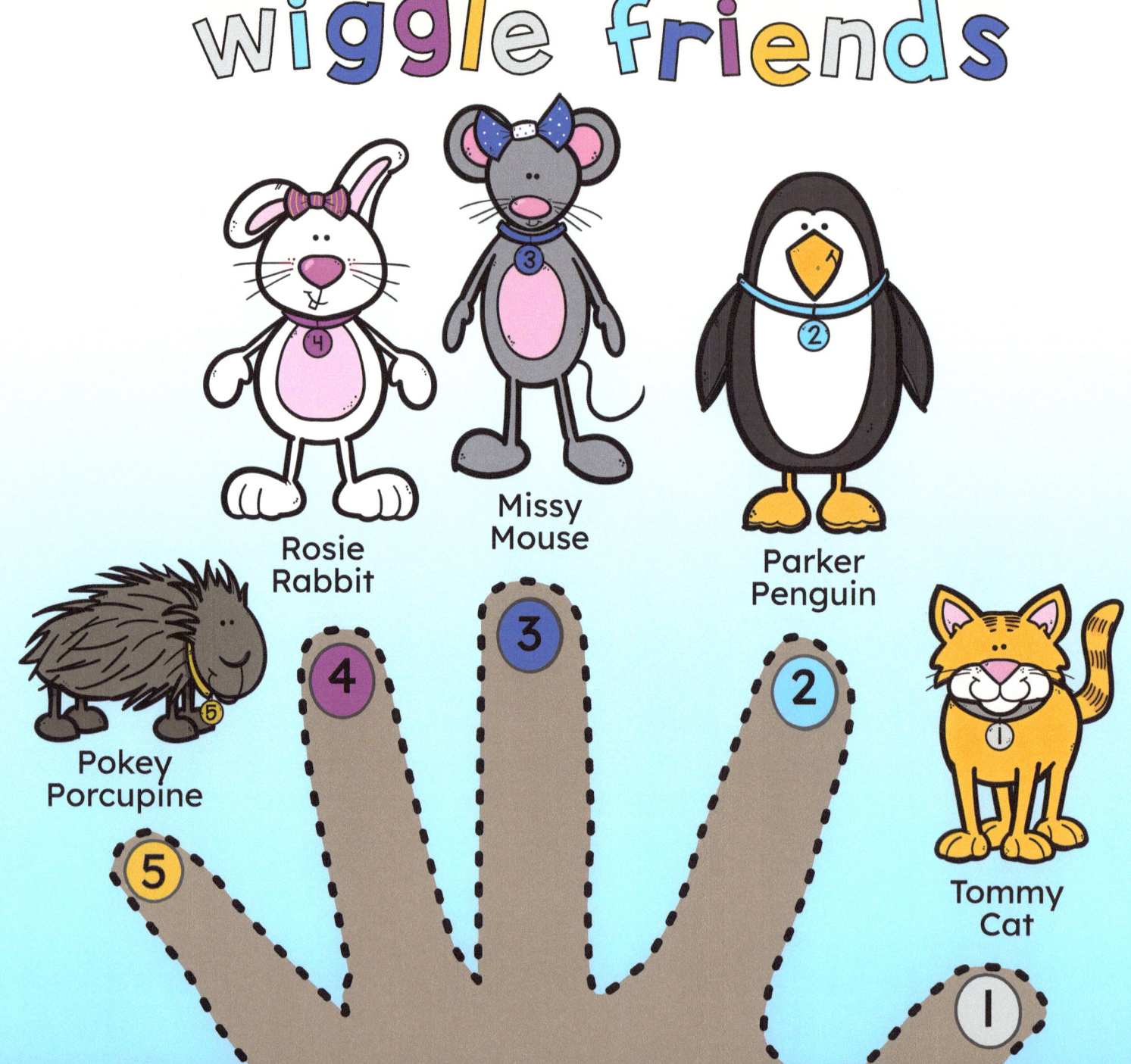

The beautiful songs make their hearts feel **warm** inside.

Every once in a while, there are a few little **rests**.

And more than a few times, Mr. Repeat will ask them all to sing their songs again...

and again...

and again.

And so, the songs and the stories
go on and on...
In that musical place called
Tiny Tinkles Town.

Follow Music Road as we sing
high and **low**.

Trace My Pretty Treble Clef

Notes that are **high** are in the sky.

Notes that are **low** are down below.

high

low Lets all sing h e l l o.

High Low Hello

Hello Mrs. Sun, hello Mrs. Sun.

Hello everyone, hello everyone.

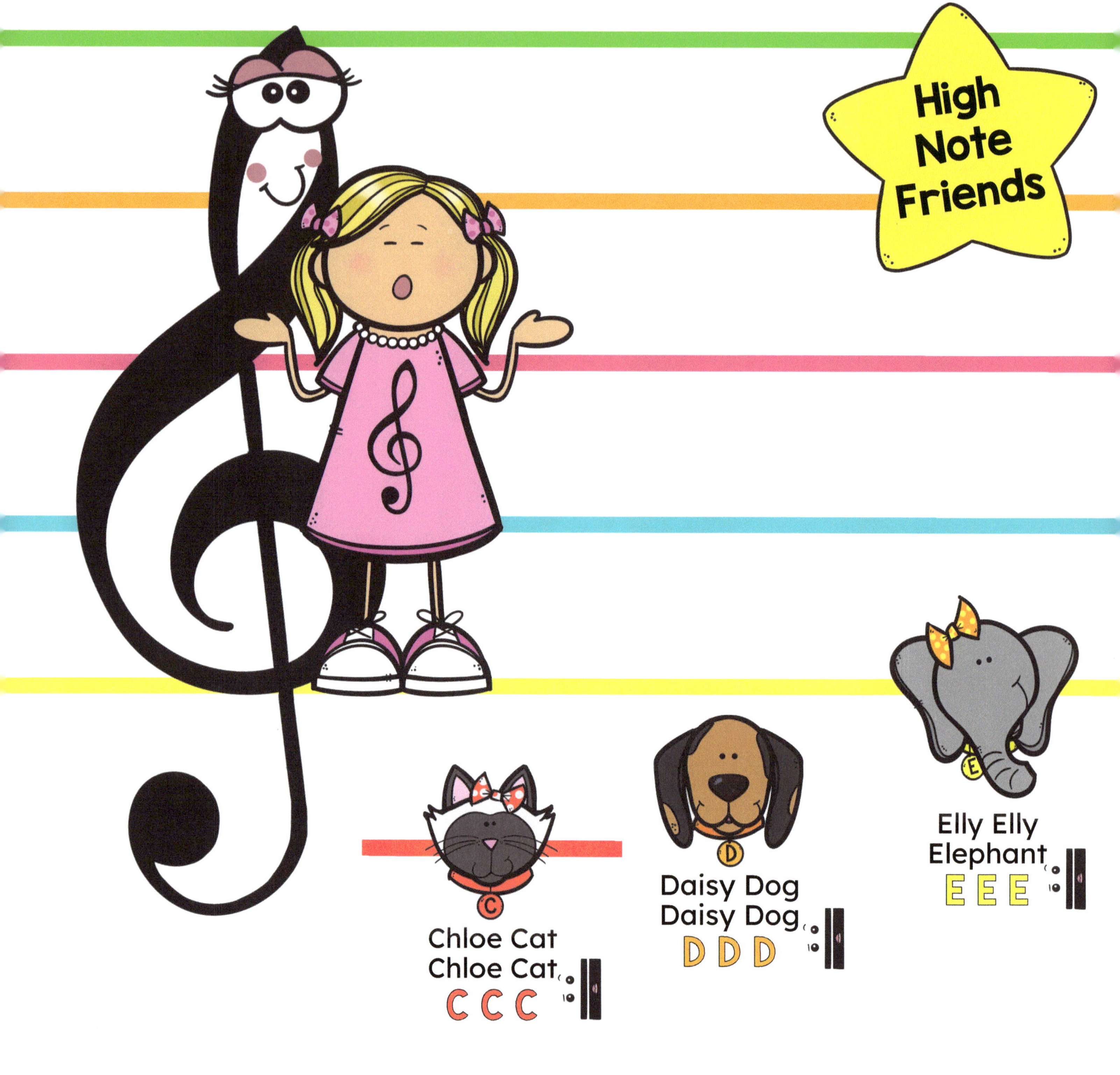

Chloe Cat
Chloe Cat
C C C

Daisy Dog
Daisy Dog
D D D

Elly Elly
Elephant
E E E

These are my HIGH Note friends!

Brownie Bear
Brownie Bear
B B B

Ally
Alligator
A A A

Gordie Goat
Gordie Goat
G G G

Franky Frog
Franky Frog
F F F

Low Note Friends

Chloe Cat
Chloe Cat
C C C

Daisy Dog
Daisy Dog
D D D

Elly Elly
Elephant
E E E

These are my **LOW Note** friends!

Game Card Cutting Instructions:

Watch a video with these instructions on our website www.tinytinkles.com

1. Cut the RED line first.
2. LAMINATE the page. (If laminating isn't an option, use a glue stick to glue each card to a sheet of card stock)
3. Cut into individual cards.
4. Tape the Tiny Tinkles Town POCKET to the INSIDE, back cover of the book. Place the tape around the sides and the bottom. Leave the top open so you can place your cards inside the pocket when not in use.

Game Ideas and Instructions:

1. SORT: Sort ALL of the game cards into piles of the same category.
2. REVIEW: Review each category carefully. How many letters, characters, or signs do you recognize? Find their names in the story if you don't remember!
3. High Low Hello Song MATCHING: Place Tina Treble and Bobby Bass and Mr. Repeat in their spots on the song page.
4. Hello All My Friends MATCHING Animals: Place each Animal Card on their spot in the music.
5. MATCHING Letters: Place each Letter Card below their spot in the music.
6. High Note Friends and Low Note Friends MATCHING Animals: Place each Animal Card on their spot in the music.
7. MATCHING Letters: Place each Letter Card below their spot in the music.
8. MATCHING Animals: Use the Song Cards to practice matching the Animal Cards and the Letter Cards.
9. Memory: Play a game with the Animal Cards and Letter Cards and see if you can make a match. Get a pair, make the animal's sound!

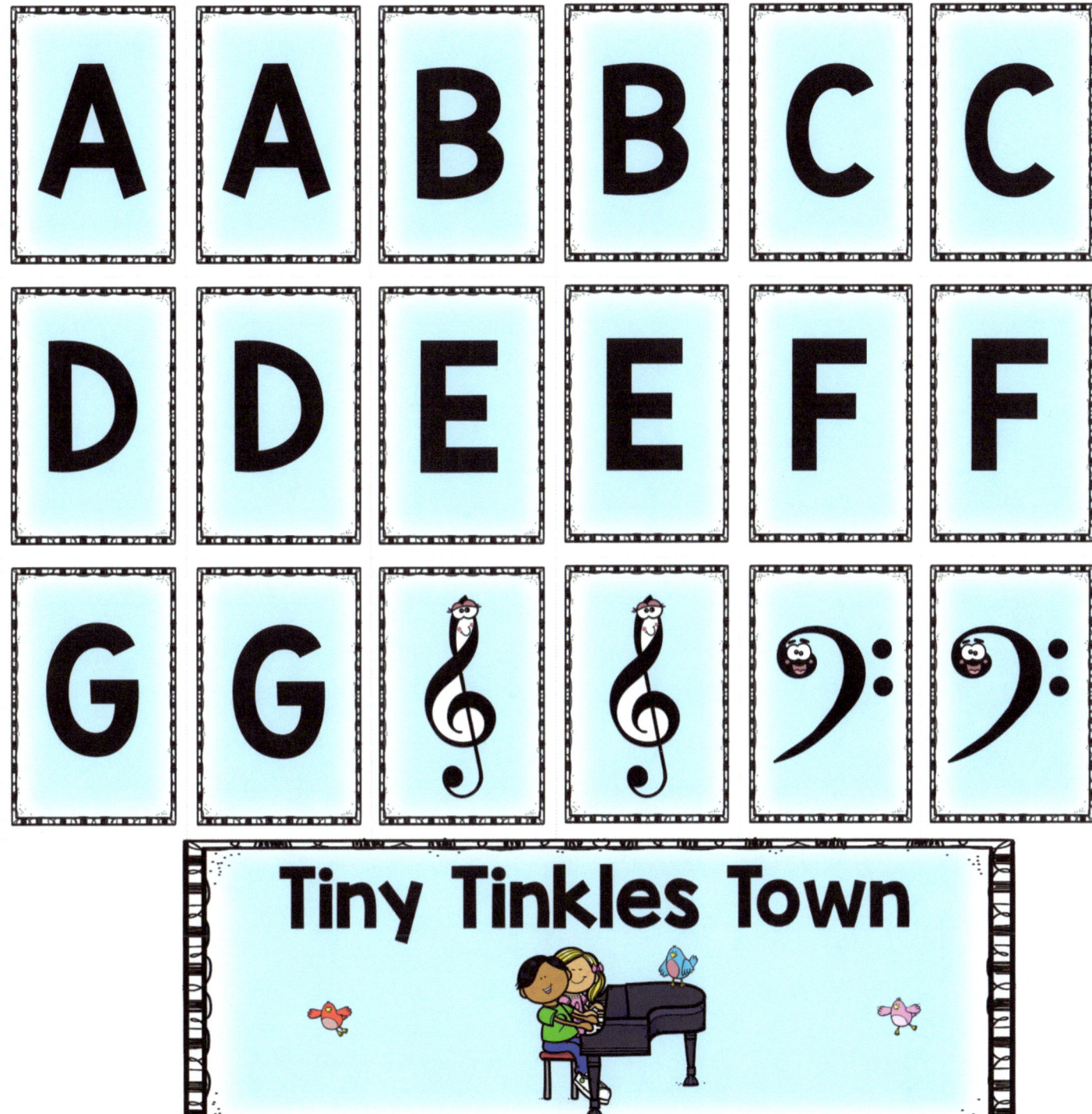

ABOUT THE CREATORS

Debra Krol is a BC Registered Music Teacher who specializes in teaching music to babies, toddlers and preschoolers. She is also a children's songwriter and author. Ms. Deb enjoys camping with her hubby, kids, and Daisy Dog, their black and tan coonhound. She loves playing piano, ukulele, guitar and most of all, singing & drawing with all of her little friends!

 Tiny Tinkles Music Studio   tinytinkles

Corinne Orazietti was a preschool and elementary teacher for many years. She saw how her whimsical illustrations added sparkle to her lessons and decided it was time to share her passion for art with others. She now works as a full-time artist at her company, Chirp Graphics, and spends her days drawing cartoon dragons and fairies.

 chirpgraphics   chirpgraphicsclipart

ABOUT THIS SERIES

The Tiny Tinkles Little Musicians Series was created to help little musicians experience the FUN of learning music. After all, the music in Tiny Tinkles Town sings in every color of the rainbow!

Every book in the Little Musician series features a Story to read, Songs to sing and play, and a ton of fun Games to play together! When a child plays to learn, they learn to play.

More books in the Little Musician Series Available in 2021.

www.ingramcontent.com/pod-product-compliance
Lightning Source LLC
Chambersburg PA
CBHW042140290426
44110CB00002B/71